MACRAMÉ ACCESSORIES

Project Book

Learn how to create a
collection of macramé accessories.

5 projects inside

Welcome to the wonderful world of macramè!

This kit has been specifically designed for adults only.

Learning a new skill is always exciting – we're here to help you get started. Macramé is an art that is incredibly easy to get into. All you need is some cord, your creativity and your hands. Once you've learnt a handful of basic knots, the possibilities are endless. Whether you want to make a handy purse, create a beautiful dream catcher, make some bespoke home decor, or anything else - it's all at your fingertips.

Let's get your creativity flowing and open your mind to this new and unlimited world.
This kit provides everything you need to make your very own macramé purse. There are also four other makes, each with a step-by-step guide for you to try.

Remember, every skill takes effort to master, so don't be disheartened if it's not perfect the first time. The most important thing is that you have fun and enjoy yourself.

Let's start your macramé journey!

KIT CONTENTS

WHAT'S INCLUDED:

- Macramé cord
- Plastic darning needle

WHAT YOU'LL NEED:

- Keyring clasp
- Earring blanks
- Scissors
- Tape measure
- Different colours and lengths of macramé cord based on the project you wish to complete.

- While we have picked our own colours feel free to use your creativity and pick your own colours of cord for the other projects (we provide the cord for the macramé purse).

BASIC KNOTS
LARKS HEAD KNOT:

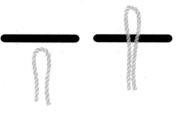

This knot is most commonly used at the beginning of a project to attach your cords onto a dowel, hoop or another cord.

1. Fold your cord in half and put the looped end over the top of the cord or dowel you are attaching it to.

2. Take the 2 ends of the cord and pull it through the loop until it's tight.

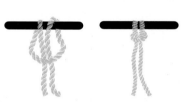

GATHERING KNOT (GK):

This knot is used to bundle cords together to create a tassel effect.

1. Cut a piece of cord long enough to wrap around your cords approx 8-10 times (depending on what your project is).

2. With your separate cord, make a loop at one end and hold it in the middle of the cords you are going to bundle.

3. Using the long end of this cord, wrap around the bundle of cords until you are happy with the size of the knot, making sure the loop stays in place but is still visible.

4. Thread the end of the wrapping cord through the loop and hold in place whilst you pull on the other end at the top of the knot. Pull the two ends tight, until the loop is hidden inside.

5. Trim both ends of the cord short and tuck in any loose threads.

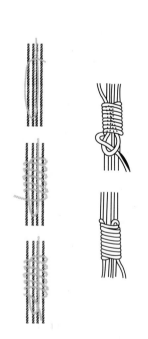

HALF HITCH & DOUBLE HITCH KNOT (HHK, DHK):

These knots will create a line across your work and are often used to create decorative diagonals and lines.

1. Take the outside cord and hold it horizontally across your work, or whatever direction you want the line to go. This is the non-working cord that the working cords will loop around.

2. Take the second cord and take it over the non-working cord and loop it through the hole.

3. Pull on the working strand to secure the knot. This is 1 half hitch knot.

4. To create a double half hitch, repeat the single half hitch knot with the same working cord.

SQUARE KNOT (SQK):

This is a super versatile knot that can be found in lots of macramé projects.

1. Each square knot is made using 4 cords. Take the first cord and make an L shape that crosses in front of cords 2 & 3 and behind the 4th cord.

2.Take the 4th cord up behind cords 2 & 3 and back through the L shape made with the first cord.

3. Pull cords 1 and 4 tight until the knot is pushed to the top of your work.

4. Repeat steps 1-3 in reverse, using the 4th cord to make a backwards L.

WARNINGS!

All the makes included in this book are designed specifically for adults.

When working with needles and cord ensure you keep them in a safe place e.g. box in your workplace. Never put needles or cord in your mouth. Keep all needlework in the packaging when not working. Do not put cord around your neck.

Keep the sharp end of the needle away from you and your eyes at all times.

Keep all materials and finished products out of the reach of children.

MACRAMÉ PURSE

MACRAMÉ PURSE

Using the contents included in this kit, create your very own boho themed macramé purse.

KIT CONTENTS

· Macramé cord
· Plastic darning needle

YOU WILL NEED

· Scissors
· Tape measure
· Comb

METHOD

1. Cut the cord into equal 2m lengths - you should end up with 25 lengths of cord.

2. Place one cord horizontally across your working space. This will be your mounting string.

Top tip- tape this down to your working space as it will be easier to work with if it has some tension.

3. Taking 20 cords, fold each in half and attach to the horizontal cord with a LHK.

4. Working from left to right, make a SqK using strings 1-4.

5. Continue to do this with each group of 4 strings until you reach the end of the row.

6. Once again, working from left to right, skip strings 1&2 and make a SqK with strings 3-6.

7. Continue to do this with each group of 4 strings until you reach the end of the row. You should have 2 strings left at the end of this process.

8. Repeat steps 4 - 7 until it is approximately 20cm long. We will now begin forming the "V" part.

9. Working from left to right, skip strings 1-2 and make a SqK with each group of 4 strings until you reach the end of the row, leaving the last 2 strings.

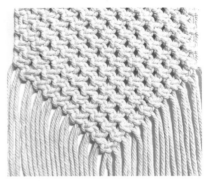

10. Working from left to right, skip strings 1-4 and make a SqK with each group of 4 strings, leaving the last 4 strings.

11. Continue this process, leaving an additional 2 strings on either end of each row as you progress until you can only do a single SqK.

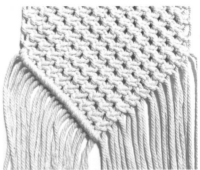

12. Take string 1 and hold it as your working string to the right. Do a DHK along the strings to the middle of the point.

13. Take string 40 - the furthest to the right - and hold it to the left. Do a DHK along the strings until you reach the middle of the point.

14. Trim the strings to approximately 7.5cm and comb out the fringe.

15. Fold the piece so that the end with the mounting string is level with the beginning of the "V" part.

16. Using the mounting string from either side, sew up the sides with the darning needle.

Well Done! Your purse is now complete.

NOTES

Use the space below to make your own personal notes on the previous project to help when you come back to make it again!

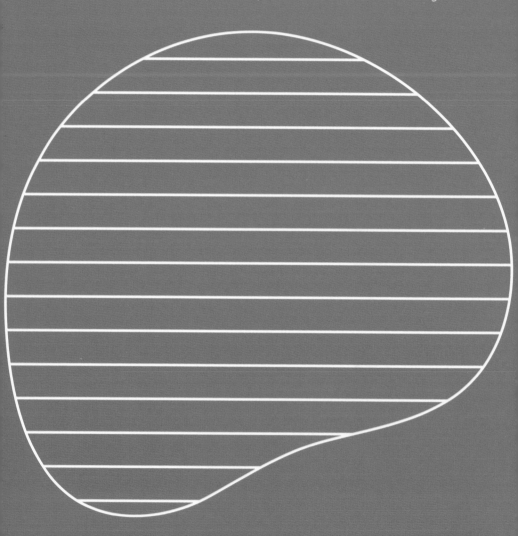

MACRAMÉ WRISTLET

MACRAMÉ WRISTLET

Create this useful wristlet to carry your cluch bag or keys on.
Personalise the colour of cord to match your style or bag.

YOU WILL NEED

·2x 2m cord
·1x 0.5m cord
·Keyring clasp
·Tape measure

METHOD

1. Taking both lengths of your 2m cord, hold them together at approximately ⅓ down the length.

2. Attach them to the keyring clasp using an LHK. You should now have two long lengths and two shorter lengths – approximately half as long as the longer strings.

3. Leaving a space of between 3-5cm, keep the two short strings in the middle, and the longer strings on the outside. Create a series of SqK's until you have approximately 5cm of cord left.

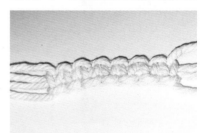

4. Fold the length of square knots over so that the beginning and end points meet.

5. Using the 5cm length of cord, bind both of these ends with a GK.

You've done it! This would make a lovely addition for the purse you've made, or attached to a set of keys to keep them safe.

NOTES

Use the space below to make your own personal notes on the previous project to help when you come back to make it again!

MACRAMÉ EARRINGS

MACRAMÉ EARRINGS

Create these fun macramé star earrings. The perfect addition to your jewellery collection.

YOU WILL NEED

- 2x Earring blanks
- 15cm lengths of cord
- Comb
- Tape measure

METHOD

1. For this project you can use an earring blank that you've purchased, or upcycle hoops that you already wear. We have used these star earrings and added our macramé to them.

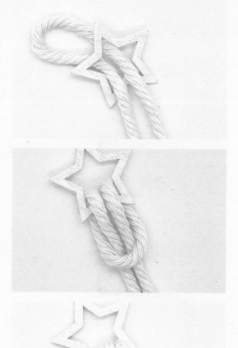

2. Fold the cord in half and attach to the earring blanks/hoops using an LHK.

3. Complete the previous step three times, (or as many times needed) to cover the base of your earrings.

4. Comb out the cords to finish your earrings.

Top tip- it's easier to use lengths longer than you intend to finish with as short lengths can be hard to tie.

NOTES

Use the space below to make your own personal notes on the previous project to help when you come back to make it again!

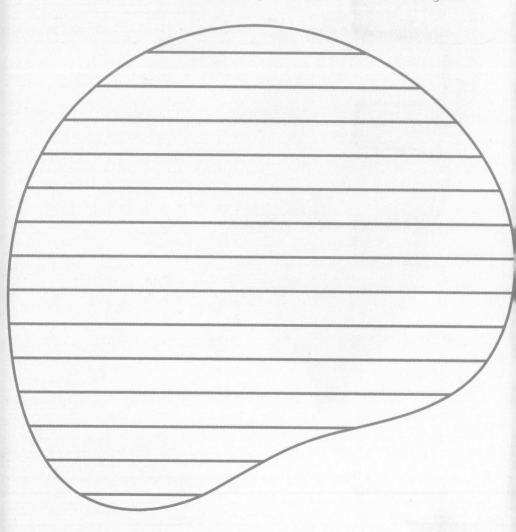

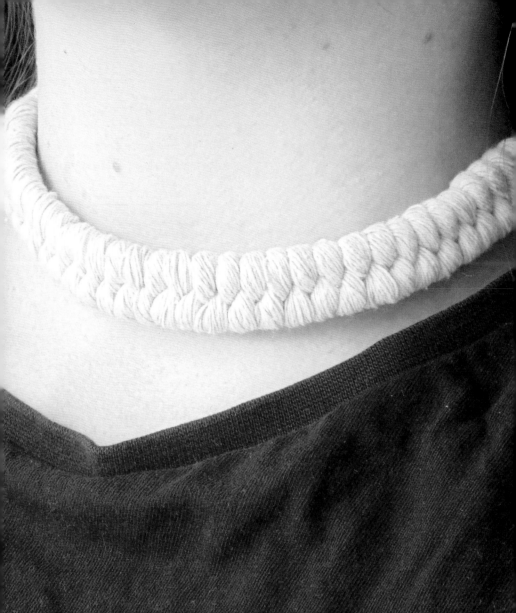

MACRAMÉ NECKLACE

MACRAMÉ NECKLACE

Follow the instructions below to make this cute, adjustable macramé necklace!

YOU WILL NEED

· 1x 3m Cord
· Scissors
·Tape measure

METHOD

1. Create a loop by twisting the yarn over itself and placing the shorter end through the loop, then out to the left.

2. Take the short tail around the top and through the loop again, then under the right hand side of the loop, over and back through the loop.

3. Do this so that you have 3 loops on either side of the main loop. Keep them snug together, then pull the long thread tight. You should now have a knot that resembles a coffee bean.

3. Trim the excess from the knot at this point.

4. Leaving approximately 40cm from the knot you've just made, create a 15cm loop.

5. Repeat the steps from above, weaving a series of figure of eights along this loop until you reach the end of the loop. At the other end of the cord, do the same knot as you made at the beginning.

6. To make your necklace adjustable, you will now create a small gather. Placing the ends of the cords in front of you, cross the right cord over the left. Then, use the left cord to create 3 loose loops around the right.

7. Now, take the same cord and place it through those loops, from the left to the right, and pull tight.

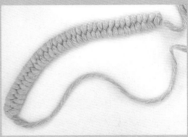

Great Job! Your necklace is now complete.

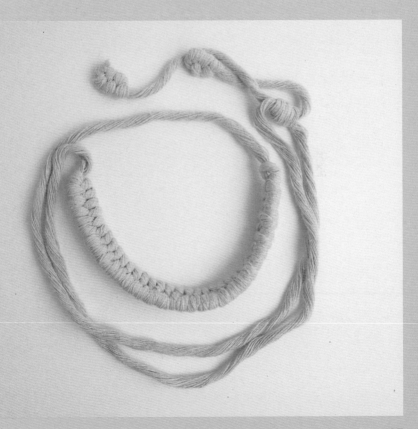

NOTES

Use the space below to make your own personal notes on the previous project to help when you come back to make it again!

41

MACRAMÉ KEYRING

MACRAMÉ KEYRING

Create this colourful macramé keyring to add to your bag, keys or anything you fancy!

YOU WILL NEED

- 3x 40cm cords in colours of your choice
- Keyring clasp
- Comb
- Tape measure

METHOD

1. Place the three strings through the keyring clasp ring.

2. Place string 1 and string 6 to the sides, then make a loop using string 2.

3. Create loops with strings 3,4, & 5, then take string 1 and thread it through the middle of these loops from the left to the right.

4. Take string 6 and thread it through the middle of these loops from the right to the left.

5. Slowly pull these strings tight.

6. Continue these steps 3 more times, then finish with a SqK.

7. Comb out the threads and trim them to your desired length.

Congratulations! What a beautiful keyring.

NOTES

Use the space below to make your own personal notes on the previous project to help when you come back to make it again!